Kingdom Mindset On Earth

God's Plan for Man

Bishop Anthony L. Taylor, Sr.

Kingdom Mindset On Earth
All Rights Reserved

No part of this book may be reproduced or copied in any form or by any means, electronic, mechanical, photocopying, recording or by any information storage or retrieval system without prior written permission of the Publisher. Inquiries should be addressed to the name and address below.

Thank you.
Published By:
Million Words Publishing, LLC
Enjoyed By You!
WORDS THAT LAST FOREVER!®
www.millionwordspublishing.com

Library of Congress Catalog Card Number:
2016910321

ISBN-10: 1-891282-08-5
ISBN-13: 978-1-891282-08-9

Kingdom Mindset On Earth
Printed in the United States of America

Table of Contents

Acknowledgements.. 5

Preface.. 6

Chapter 1
God's Original Plan — Dominion........................ 7-13

Chapter 2
Man Lost Dominion... 14-21

Chapter 3
God's Promise of Redemption............................ 22-26

Chapter 4
Dominion Restored... 27-33

Chapter 5
Sons Not Servants... 34-41

Chapter 6

The Misunderstood Message............................. 42-49

Chapter 7

The NEW Heaven and NEW Earth....................... 50-55

About the Author... 56-58

Acknowledgements...

I would like to give special thanks to my lovely wife, Elaine Taylor, who has always been my big supporter of all my endeavors for more than 28 years (Love You Babe)! Thanks to my children, Joya, Tony, Krystle, and Rhonada who allowed me to do the work of the Kingdom when it interfered with the time I could have spent with them.

Thanks to my pastor, Rev. AB Jackson, West Bethel Church, who has provided spiritual guidance for more than 20 years, and to my spiritual parents, Dr. Martin Williams and his lovely wife Pastor Lynell, Ambassadors Worship Center, Omaha, Nebraska, for taking me under their wings and allowing me to become their spiritual son. Thanks to the Late Dr. Myles Monroe for pouring out the Kingdom information during his conferences and meetings.

Also, special thanks to my Administrative Assistant, Mrs. Evone Sims, for the efforts and support and pulling the book together. Also, thanks to Alice Johnson, of Million Words Publishing, for working with me and publishing my first book. Thanks to the New Hope Church Family & Friends for trusting and believing in the Word of God.

Preface...

In *Kingdom Mindset On Earth* you will learn the concept of changing your mindset from a slave mentality to the mindset of a king, a ruler, and to have dominion over your territory. I was inspired to write this book after learning about the Kingdom of God and His mandate for mankind on earth. My heart and mind went to another level in preaching the Word of God. I was no longer the same after getting illumination for mankind's purpose on earth. God reveals so much to me through reading and studying His Word as well as through His Holy Spirit. My heart is yearning to share this knowledge with the world. It's been a struggle in writing this book because I didn't consider myself a writer, but as I began to write, I realized that writing was more than just putting information on paper, it also involves my desire to bring truth to God's people regarding His plan for mankind to live an abundant life and to have sovereign power here on earth.

Chapter 1
God's Original Plan — Dominion

Genesis 1:26: Then God said, "Let Us make man in Our image, according to Our likeness; let them have <u>dominion</u> over the fish of the sea, over the birds of the air, and over the cattle, over all the earth and over every creeping thing that creeps on the earth."

This particular scripture identifies that God created man to be like Him. God the Father, the Son, and the Holy Ghost had a conversation saying, "Let Us make man in Our image, according to Our likeness." Let Us pay close attention to the passage, **"Our image and Our likeness,"** meaning that when man was created, he was created just like God, in His image, and exactly the way God wanted man to be. In order to understand the meaning "In God's image," you must know His image. Let me explain; first of all God is a Ruler, a King, and a Creator that has dominion over everything He created with the Words of His mouth by speaking things into existence. Therefore, when He said, "Let Us make man in our image," He was just saying let Us create a man to be like Us; to be a ruler, to be a king. A ruler to simply rule his territory; he has dominion over all that is within his area. Dominion simply means to rule, control, and to have sovereign power!!!

After the conversation of making man was finished, God said, "Let them (meaning mankind), have dominion over the fish of the sea, over the birds of the air, and over the cattle, <u>over all the earth</u> and over every creeping thing that creeps on the earth" (Genesis 1:26). God was just stating let them (man) have control/dominion over all the creations (Psalm 8:6).

> **Genesis 2:7: And the Lord God formed man of the dust of the ground, and breathed into his nostrils the breath of life, and man became a living soul.**

In Genesis 1:26, after God said let us make man in our image; He continues the process of making man. In Genesis 2:7, He formed man from the dust of the ground and breathed into man's nostrils the breath of life. God breathed His DNA into man's nostrils and at that point, man became a living soul. Consequently, man took on the same characteristics of God; having the same potential and capabilities of God the Father, who is a King/Ruler. Psalm 82:6 says, "I have said, Ye are gods; and all of you are children of the most High." Notice in this passage He refers to the small letter "g" identifying His children as small gods. It is a known fact that when something is made in the same image of its maker, it takes on the same characteristics of its creator. Therefore, when God made man in His image, man became like God. Just as God is a King and rules heaven, His plan was for man to be a king and to rule/govern the earth; to make earth resemble heaven; to be in peace and harmony with all of His creation. God never intended for man to die, go to heaven, live there eternally, and walk around heaven all day with streets paved with gold, as one song states. God's ultimate plan was for man to live on earth and subdue it. Man's rulership consisted of the fish of the sea, the birds, the cattle, and all creeping things over the whole earth. Mankind is not considered a creeping thing, bird, fish or cattle therefore, God never intended for man to have dominion over another man. He wants a kingdom of priests to rule as He purposed us in the beginning. In Psalm 115:16, the Word of God states that the highest heavens belong to the LORD, but the earth has he given to man.

God's plan was to share His rulership with His sons, the priests of the earth, in a different location, but by the same Spirit. He gave man an inheritance called the kingdom. Man's job was to make earth a model after heaven. God wanted to get His glory and nature on earth through the creation of His sons. If this then is the case and I agree, according to Psalm 8:1-5, God has given man dominion over all His creation by His hands. Therefore, whatever happens on the earth is mankind's fault. God is not in control of everything neither is the devil according to Genesis 1:26, Psalm 115:15, and Psalm 8:1-5. If God was in control the world would have been fixed a long time ago because He is not the author of confusion, and the earth is full of confusion. The winds don't know how hard to blow so they create tornados and hurricanes; the waters have no idea when to stop, so they flood cities. These events use to obey the commands of man's voice until he lost control. For example, Jesus was asleep in the ship and His disciples asked Him, "Cares not that we perish?" Jesus woke from His sleep and rebuked the wind and calmed the sea.

    If God's was in control and it was His will, do you think Jesus would go against the Father? Hmm, of course not! If the devil was in control of everything, he would not allow us to study God's Word or to be in fellowship with one another ever, so the problem lies with mankind whom God gave dominion!!! Man has been shifting the blame since the day they were kicked out the Garden of Eden. Remember, when God asked Adam, Where art thou when they hid themselves because of their disobedience?

> **Genesis 3:12-13: And the man said, The woman whom thou gavest to be with me, she gave me of the tree, and I did eat. And the LORD God said unto the woman, What is this that thou hast done? And the woman said, The serpent beguiled me, and I did eat.**

The earth looks the way it does because mankind has made it this way and we keep praying to God to fix it and God is waiting on the sons of God to come forth that He may empower them to straighten things out.

Kingdom Beliefs

1. Then God said, "Let Us make _____ in Our _____, according to Our _____."

2. What was man suppose to have rule over?
   a. Himself   b. Satan   c. God   d. Earth

3. Does God rule the earth? ☐ Yes   ☐ No

4. Whose image was man made from? _____

5. Define Dominion: _____
   _____
   _____

6. Psalm 8:1-5 states that God has given man _____ over all His creations.

7. The Lord God formed man from the _____ of the ground and _____ his nostril the breath of _____.

8. In Psalm 115:16 states that the Heavens even the heavens belong to God, but the earth has He given to _____.

God's Original Plan — Dominion

Kingdom Notes

Chapter 2
Man Lost Dominion

Genesis 3:1-5: Now the serpent was more subtil than any beast of the field which the LORD God had made. And he said unto the woman, Yea, hath God said, Ye shall not eat of every tree of the garden? And the woman said unto the serpent, We may eat of the fruit of the trees of the garden: But of the fruit of the tree which is in the midst of the garden, God hath said, Ye shall not eat of it, neither shall ye touch it, lest ye die. And the serpent said unto the woman, Ye shall not surely die: For God doth know that in the day ye eat thereof, then your eyes shall be opened, and ye shall be as gods, knowing good and evil.

As man walks with God, he should be mindful of the voices he listens to for the voice of the enemy can be very deceptive having one to believe that the Lord is talking. Not only does the enemy have a good sounding voice, he transforms himself to look good, smell good, and use cunning words. Remember that the serpent (the devil) was more subtle than any creature ever made. As he began to speak he got Eve's attention immediately by using the word of God saying (paraphrasing) *"Hey there good looking, did God say you cannot eat of every tree in the garden?"* Apparently, the woman was so overwhelmed she even twisted God's words herself by saying, "Ye shall not eat of it; nor touch it" (Genesis 4:3). The Bible does not mention anything about not touching the tree, it only mentioned not to eat from one specific tree—the tree of knowledge of good and evil.

When God gives instructions they are clear and precise; just as He said to Adam in Genesis 2:16-17, "And the Lord God commanded the man, saying, Of every tree of the garden thou mayest freely eat: But of the tree of the knowledge of good and evil, thou shalt not eat of it: for in the day that thou eatest thereof thou shalt surely die." God gives instructions on what things man can eat, just as in today's society, God speaks to man through the Holy Spirit and His Word. Man often loses focus on what God has to say and begins to listen to an outside source. Not only does God speak through man directly, He also speaks through His leader (the pastor) with instructions through vision and dreams. However, just as it was during the time of Adam and Eve, we rather listen to an outside source other than what the man of God has to say. No doubt, Satan began to speak to the woman by telling her with his good sounding words that she will not surly die if she ate of the tree of knowledge. He even went so far as to say that God doesn't want her to eat because she would become like Him (God) knowing good and evil. Apparently, she did not realize that she was already like God because she was made in His image, and His likeness (Genesis, 1:26). When

God breathed His DNA into the nostril of man, He became a living soul, being just like His creator, God (Genesis 2:7).

If you would read in the book of Genesis 3:6-8, you find that the woman saw that the tree was good for food as well as pleasant to the eyes. It was over once she realized how good the tree looked and how it quenched her hunger; not only did she eat, but also gave to her husband to eat; who stood by her side as the devil spoke. Maybe the devil temporarily blinded Adam, plugged his ears, or put him in a deep sleep while he communicated with Eve. I am not quite sure why Adam stood there during this conversation between the woman and the devil, but he sold out on what God gave him for a temporary pleasure. Naturally, immediately after they ate from the tree of knowledge their eyes became opened, and they were no longer innocent. Adam and Eve saw themselves in a different light knowing they were naked, and began to cover themselves with fig leaves and aprons. They had lost the covering of God and what the Father had given them (dominion). They no longer had the respect or the authority over the earth and creation that God had given them. Adam and Eve also lost their priestly garment and now had to cover themselves with fig leaves. The glory and honor God crowned them with in Psalm 8:5 were now lost, and you cannot cover up or replace God's glory and honor. What

Adam actually did was commit treason. He declared independence from His country, Heaven where God rules. God wanted to get His nature and culture in the earth through His family Adam and Eve, but they didn't follow the instructions from their home government resulting in loss of authority and dominion from God, the Father, King, and Governor. Also, because of this all creation has rebelled against the one responsible for it, Adam!

    An excellent comparison to Adam and Eve covering themselves is just like God's people of today after making a mistake or sinning, people tend to stray away from God or the house of God. Usually, they feel as if though they have let God down and He won't hear them because of their mistakes or their sins. Remember, Adam and Eve knew no sin. Also, take into consideration that God met with Adam in the cool of the day, and communicated with him, but this particular day when they heard God coming in the cool of the day, they hid themselves. Adam had no idea of the consequences he would face by going against God's Word; not only did his decision affect him and Eve, it affected the entire creation. Adam's decision has caused every man and woman born in the world to have a sinful nature, except Jesus. It's like a parent with a disease that passes it to all their children. Of course, most of the children in the world do not understand why things are the way they are neither why they act certain ways against themselves and one another. Here is a breakdown of the story of what happened when they ate from the forbidden tree:

- ✟ Adam heard God's voice and was afraid.
- ✟ Adam knew they were naked.
- ✟ Adam hid themselves from God.
- ✟ God asked Adam where art thou.
- ✟ Adam answered, "Heard thy voice, hid myself,"
- ✟ Adam blamed the woman; the woman blamed the serpent.
- ✟ Enmity between the woman and serpent, and his seed and her seed.
- ✟ Man kicked out of the garden.
- ✟ Cherubim and a flaming sword protecting the garden so they couldn't return.

Adam has now lost dominion. If you noticed, Adam had power over death, sin, animals, wind, sea, and over all the earth; so if Adam had this power, whatever happens on earth is Adam and his children's fault, and not God's or Satan's. Since God had given this dominion to Adam in the beginning (Genesis 1:26, Psalm 8:5) over the earth, then Adam ruled it with his voice. Whatever Adam called the animal, that's what it was. Death and sin had no power over Adam until he disobeyed God, then he gave life to death and sin under the authority of Satan.

Kingdom Beliefs

1. Man could eat of every tree of the garden except for the tree of _____ and He said thou shalt not eat of it or you will surely _____.

2. Adam heard the voice of God in the cool of the night.
   __True   __False

3. Adam did not know he was naked after he ate from the tree.
   __True   __False

4. Adam hid himself from God before he ate from the tree of knowledge of good and evil.
   __True   __False

5. Did God ask Adam where art thou?
   __True   __False

6. Man remained in the garden after eating of the tree.
   __True   __False

7. Flaming sword protecting the garden to keep man in.
   __True   __False

8. Who did Adam blame for his mistake?
   __ The serpent   __ The woman   __ God

9. Who did the woman blame?
   __ God   __ The serpent   __ Adam

10. God put enmity between the _____?
    __ The woman and Satan   __ Adam and Eve

Kingdom Mindset On Earth

Kingdom Notes

Chapter 3
God's Promise of Redemption

Genesis 3:15: And I will put enmity between thee and the woman, and between thy seed and her seed; it shall crush thy head, and thou shalt bruise his heel.

At this point God's plans were to redeem man by sending His son, Jesus, even though Adam gave his seat of power to Satan, God had a plan for redeeming it back for His children. Every world system, every soul that wants to be, and every kingdom that Satan had; God wants it back. So, He promised that in the fullness of time He would send His Son, our Elder Brother, our King of Kings, our Lord of Lords; the Savior of the world who would come and redeem it back for us. But, the sad part about the church in general is most are just happy with Jesus saving us and becoming our Savior. However, He's done so much more than that, He not only quickened our spirit to keep us from the lake of the fire (Roman 10:9), but He also gave us power that Adam lost in the garden.

Jesus came to the earth just like us (full mankind), but without a natural man producing him. He grew up like a normal kid, worked like a normal man—ate, slept, prayed, got hungry, and tired just like the rest of mankind, so He was no different than any mere man, except for His conception was not by Joseph; His earthly father, but by the Holy Ghost, and His earthly mother, Mary!!! Jesus is three part being as we are, and He is a spirit in a body with a soul. We are a spirit with a soul in a body. Now, if this Holy Spirit lives in your body changing your natural spirit to be conformed to the son of God's spirit, and by the renewing of your mind, then you should be like the Redeemer. Simply put, we that are born again according to the Word of God has the same potential of Jesus. As a matter of fact, Jesus said to go preach the kingdom of heaven, heal the sick, cleanse the leper, and raise the dead.

God has shown all His intention to send a redeemer down through history. He gave many typologies in the Old Testament about Jesus, the son of God coming. One example was when God told Abraham to sacrifice His Son on the mountain and Abraham obeyed (Genesis 22:2-6). Another example was the sacrifice of animals through the shedding of their blood which was the typology of Christ being sacrificed for our sins.

God shows us many ways of His Son's coming even with the rock that Moses hit the first time as a whipping of Christ going to Calvary. Moses was supposed to speak to the rock the second time, but he hit the rock instead causing God to become angry with him. It also caused him not to lead the people in the Promise Land. There are so many examples in history before Christ's coming the first time. However, I can't name them all, but one of my favorites is Isaiah 53:5, "But He was wounded for our transgressions; He was bruised for our iniquities, the chastisement of our peace was upon Him; and with His stripes we are healed."

I am so glad God is not a man that He shall lie. If He says a thing, it shall come to pass. He is the only one who knows the future just like it should happen, and the only one who can forgive the pass before it becomes the pass. Revelation 13:8 states, "And all that dwell upon the earth shall worship Him, whose names are not written in the book of life of the Lamb slain from the foundation of the world." Because God will not allow Satan to have anything that He creates, God provided a way for His children, and all of God's promises are Yea and Amen.

God Himself showed grace and mercy when He killed the first animal to cover Adam and Eve with a temporary cover. This symbolizes the sacrifice of the coming redeemer. The promised redeemer came by way of a miracle, the Virgin Mary. She was favored by God and used as a vehicle to bring the Messiah into the world. Satan himself knew this promise was coming so he was waiting and tried several times to stop it, but what God says always shall come true.

Kingdom Mindset On Earth

Kingdom Beliefs

1. What were God's plans for redeeming the earth? _____
   _____
   _____
   _____

2. And I will put _____ between thee and the _____ and between thy _____ and her seed; it shall _____ thy head and thou shalt bruise his _____. (Genesis 3:15)

3. God promised that in the _____ of time _____ would send His _____ to redeem the kingdom back for his children.

4. God shows us many ways of His _____ coming even with the rock that _____ hit the first time as a beating of _____ going to _____.

God's Promise of Redemption

Kingdom Notes

Chapter 4
Dominion Restored

Jesus came to buy back that which was lost by man (Adam) in the Garden of Eden. God planted man in the garden to rule the earth, but of course man lost dominion when he disobeyed God's commandment and ate from the tree of the knowledge of good and evil. Therefore, in order for man to get control of earth again, God had to send His son Jesus to purchase it back. Man never had ownership of heaven, only rulership of the earth.

When Jesus came to this earth, He came into a religious system that held people in bondage to what was called the law of man. The political environment was the Roman Empire which was one of the most powerful and dominating governments of all times. During Jesus life on earth He owned nothing even though He was sent by God, the Father, and He Himself was God in flesh, blood, and body. He had given up all of those attributes in order to accomplish a work that was in the heart of the Father—to restore that which was lost. While He was accomplishing this task, Jesus was also modeling for humanity what our life is to be like as God created us with authority over the creation having dominion over all things.

Jesus revolution was to destroy the stronghold of the kingdom of darkness and restore humanity's access to the kingdom of God. This is the reason why John the Baptist primary message was "Repent for the kingdom of God is at hand." John was the forerunner for Jesus. He was introducing what Jesus was to bring back to mankind. John was merely saying to the people, "turn away from the darkness, change your religious way of thinking, and your self-righteous way of acting." In other words, stop your every Sunday morning judgment in the church, your judging people to hell, your preaching one thing and living another, and your faithless doctrine, and follow Him. By following Him, He will show you how to gain access to the Kingdom of God for it is right here close at hand. Never did He preach to the multitude about His death, burial, and resurrection.

The only time Jesus talked about His death, burial, and resurrection was when He told His disciples it is better for them if He go. His focus was to go and do the will of His Father, for this is why He was sent. Please take note that the death of Jesus and His resurrection is important since it is a means to an end. You need that in order to be in the kingdom of God just like He told Nicodemus in John 3. Jesus knew His role was to die in order to restore the lost kingdom to man. In Matthew 18:11, when it said that the son of Man came to save that which was lost, it was specifically speaking of restoring the dominion (rulership) that Adam lost back in the Garden of Eden.

Most religious organizations, such as the church, say that it was only the people who are lost in sin and need to be saved. Only, if that was the case, then scripture would have not been so precise to say that which was lost, it would have read those who were lost as well. If Jesus could save the system of the world, that would save the people in the world. The word "save" is a Greek word "sozo," which means to save from destruction, save something in its entirety, or to restore to completeness. Sozo also means to deliver from the consequences of our fallen nature called **SIN**—the denial to allow God to be God in your life.

Jesus had to accomplish what was in the heart of the Father, which was to return earth to its original condition that which was lost. He was to restore completely what had been lost, and when He died on the cross, He cried out "**IT IS FINISHED!**" Jesus had accomplished the purpose He had been sent to do. He had returned back to humanity the keys to put the earth back in its original condition before everything was lost. Jesus had redeemed humanity from under the control of sin. He had reconciled humanity to fellowship with God. Jesus restored humanity to a state of glory by giving them His righteousness as a gift of His incredible love. He restored man's dominion over the earth, and did much, much more than we can ever imagine.

In the city of St. Louis if someone ever had a car stolen, and it was towed to the impound yard, even though the car was theirs, they had to buy it out of the impound yard. That is what Jesus did, because even though the earth is the Lord's and the fullness thereof, and though He left mankind in control of it, Satan got a hold of the control. Jesus had to buy back (the systems of the world) by redeeming it at the cross. Luke 4:4-6: "And Jesus answered him, saying, It is written, That man shall not live by bread alone, but by every word of God. And the devil, taking him up into an high mountain, shewed unto him all the kingdoms of the world in a moment of time. And the devil said unto him, All this power will I give thee, and the glory of them: for that is delivered unto me; and to whomsoever I will I give it."

When this happened, Jesus restored man back to his original position, which is dominion over the earth, not heaven, which most churches preach. Adam never lost heaven so therefore if Jesus was restoring mankind, it had to be back to the same place he lost and that is dominion over the earth.

Kingdom Beliefs

1. In order for _____ to get control of earth again; _____ had to send His son Jesus to _____ it back.

2. Man always had ownership of heaven, and rulership of the earth.
   __True __False

3. God created us, with _____ over the creation having _____ over all things.

4. John the Baptist primary message was "_____ for the kingdom of God is at hand."

5. Never did He preach to the multitude about His death, burial, and resurrection.
   __True __False

6. If Jesus could save the system of the world, that would save the people in the world.
   __True __False

7. The word "save" is a Greek word "sozo," which means? _____
   _____

8. Jesus had reconciled humanity to fellowship with Satan.
   __True   __False

Dominion Restored

Kingdom Notes

Chapter 5
<u>Sons Not Servants</u>

Galatians 4:4-7: But when the fullness of the time was come, God sent forth his Son, made of a woman, made under the law. To redeem them that were under the law, that we might receive the adoption of sons. And because ye are sons, God hath sent forth the Spirit of his Son into your hearts, crying, Abba, Father. Wherefore thou art no more a servant, but a son; and if a son, then an heir of God through Christ.

When God sent Jesus to redeem what man had lost, Jesus did everything He needed to do. He said, "Father, it is finished." He did this over 2,000 years ago!!! So what's wrong with our world today? The problem may not be what you think. It's not so much as our local government, not condemnation, not resources, or even sin; the bottom line of the problem is that the majority of people today do not identify with God as their Father. They relate to Him as being slaves or servants, and not sons. That is, they have a parentless spirit. Most people think like the son who left home (prodigal son) after receiving his inheritance and blowing it on riotous living saying, "Make me a hired servant for I'm not worthy to be called thy son," but this is part of the work that Jesus did on the cross. He bought back that privilege so we can become sons again if we believe and receive the love of God, the Father.

This is where both grace and mercy comes in and gives us provision of our loving Father. Grace He gives us, which is an unmerited favor—things we don't deserve. Mercy He gives us, which is not giving us what we deserve. If people would change their way of thinking and live life as the kings and queens He made us, then life more abundantly will come.

> **Romans 12:1-3: I beseech you therefore, brethren, by the mercies of God, that ye present your bodies a living sacrifice, holy, acceptable unto God, which is your reasonable service. And be not conformed to this world: but be ye transformed by the renewing of your mind, that ye may prove what is that good, and acceptable, and perfect, will of God. For I say, through the grace given unto me, to every man that is among you, not to think of himself more highly than he ought to think; but to think soberly, according as God hath dealt to every man the measure of faith.**

There may be only two kinds of people in the world: sons and servants. The first Adam made you a servant, but the second Adam (Jesus) made you a son. Which are you? Your choice!! The devil, which is an enemy of God the Father, wants to get you confused about your identity. He tries to put doubt in your mind by asking, "If you are the Son of God . . ." He tried that on Jesus, but Jesus knew who He was, no doubt and always quoted what was written. If you listen to the devil long enough he will try to put doubt in your mind like he did Adam and Eve. "For God doth know that in the day ye eat thereof, then your eyes shall be opened, and ye shall be as gods, knowing good and evil" (Genesis 3:5). They were already gods because they were created in the image and likeness of God. "I have said, Ye are gods; and all of you are children of the most High" (Psalm 82:6).

The enemy wants to make you uncertain about your sonship to the extent that you have an orphan spirit. So many people, especially in the church, are victims of identity theft! I urge you not to allow the devil to run off with your birth certificates, he is a liar, and a thief. Scripture says he comes to steal, kill, and destroy. If you serve God who is your best friend, you are first and foremost a son of God, and this applies equally to the ladies, for we are all one in Christ (Galatians 3:28).

God did not create us to be servants/slaves because we were created out of Himself, therefore, we are His children, and not His servants. However, because of Adam's sin we took on a servant or slave mentality. God made Adam to rule over all the earth, fish of the sea, fowls of the air, all creeping things, the wind, the water, hatred, sin, and death. Hatred, sin, and death has always existed, but had no power or authority over mankind. If you notice when God gave Adam dominion he named everything (Genesis 2:20), and everything was ruled by his voice. In other words, Adam could just say what he wanted and it was.

God gave Adam just what he had in heaven, but Adam rule was on the earth. God told Adam, "look, you have control over all this on earth, but if you mess up that which you rule, you will become prohibited, and you won't be able to control it, it will control you!!!" So, Adam (mankind), God's son, the ruler, became ruled as a servant and a slave. He lost his voice of authority over creation, sin, and death. If you can imagine being there when death and the animals said to Adam, "You can't tell me what to do; you didn't even obey your Father. You brought all of this confusion in your own domain, the earth." So sin and death have their moments of running wild in our lives with the help of other circumstances, such as foreign substances we put in our body, growing older, and how we physically abuse the body. This is why most people have a slave or servant mentality, not realizing being created in the image of God is powerful. God is not a servant or a slave, therefore, because we are created in His image and likeness, we should think like Him.

He makes us His sons and daughters and freely gives us all good things. When we ask for His forgiveness, He wipes away our sins and forgets it ever happened. John 15:15 states, "Henceforth I call you not servants; for the servant knoweth not what his lord doeth: but I have called you friends; for all things that I have heard of my Father I have made known unto you."

If you would look at the parable of the lost son, you will notice the fact that the son left his father's care, his house, and his rules, and started living like a servant, but when he thought about the consequences of his actions and came to himself he said:

> **Luke 15:17-19:** . . . **"How many hired servants of my father's have bread enough and to spare, and I perish with hunger! I will arise and go to my father, and will say unto him, Father, I have sinned against heaven, and before thee, And am no more worthy to be called thy son: make me as one of thy hired servants."** **And he arose, and came to his father.**

However, when he went to his father, he refused to call his son a servant or a slave, and he restored him back to his rightful position. When we come back to the Father through Jesus Christ, the son by faith, then we have the same spirit and can say, "Abba Father," because we are no longer called a servant, but a son. If you are a son you need to think like a son. We need to think like royalty because we are kings and queens, not servants. Let me remind you that servants have no inheritance to the Father's wealth.

Kingdom Beliefs

1. Most people _____ to God as _____ or _____ and not son.

2. Jesus bought back that _____ so we can become _____ again if we believe and receive the love of _____ the Father.

3. God gives us _____ which is unmerited _____ of things we don't deserve.

4. There may be only two kinds of people in the world: _____ and _____. The first Adam made you a servant but the second Adam (Jesus) made you a _____.

5. God did not create us to _____/_____ because we were created out of Himself.

6. God is not a servant or a slave.
   __True   __False

Kingdom Mindset On Earth

Kingdom Notes

Chapter 6
The Misunderstood Message

In the Bible there are several typologies that points to the coming of our Lord Jesus Christ the King. For example, in the Old Testament Genesis 22:2, when God tells Abraham to take now thy son, thine only son Isaac, whom thou lovest, and get thee into the land of Moriah; and offer him there for a burnt offering upon one of the mountains which I will tell thee. Abraham did what God told him until God intervened. This is an example of how God gave up His only begotten son. But the misunderstanding is that Abraham had more than one son at the time, So does God. Hmmm (Selah). Another example is when the father, Abraham, sent out his servant to choose a bride for his son. The servant took gifts to the bride just like the Holy Ghost gives gift to the church, the bride of Christ. There are so many examples throughout the Bible that refer to our King's coming.

As for the message that the church has so greatly misunderstood is the idea that God, the Father, is trying to get to us and the world system is the message about a Father (Elohim), His children, and their inheritance. So the Father sent His son Jesus, to bring us the message that He gave Adam in the beginning. But to prepare us for the news, He sent John the Baptist to get our minds ready for the coming of the One who would restore back to us what Adam lost, and that is dominion over the creations by the Father. John's message was to repent for the kingdom of heaven was near. This simply means the way you have been thinking is off base. You are children of a King, but you think like slaves, so repent, for your power and control is near. That was the message that John shared everywhere he went. John introduced us to the One (Jesus) who would bring the kingdom.

When John saw Jesus he said, "Behold the Lamb of God." The next day two of John's disciples heard Jesus speak, and they followed Jesus. Then Jesus turned and saw them following Him, and saith unto them, "What seek ye?" They said, "The Master, King, Rabbi, the Messiah, the One who will show us the Father's way, and the way you speak with power and authority we know you can show us." Jesus then informed them to follow Him.

Jesus took twelve men, taught them, and showed them the way of the Father. As they followed Him, hung around Him, watched Him, asked Him questions, He began teaching them about the kingdom that the Father had for us since the foundation of the world by doing what He spoke about. Jesus came to speak to us about a kingdom. He came to show us how the kingdom works and to give back to us the power that Adam lost. This was God's intention in the beginning and

God always gets what He said!!! Whatever he said shall come to pass. So, the message that Jesus taught His disciples was about the kingdom that He brought to them and the kingdom to come. When He was teaching them, first He said, "Follow me," and He showed them what to do. Secondly, He said, "Do as I do," and thirdly He said, "Now you go." When Jesus had fasted for forty days after He was hungry the devil tried to tempt Him, but Jesus kept referring back to what His government had written. After that was over Luke 4:43 states, "And he said unto his disciples, I must preach the kingdom of God to other cities also: for therefore am I sent." He had a message when he came to earth. He did not have to make up one because it was the one from the Father that sent Him. He gave this message to his followers.

> **Matthew 10:7-8: And as ye go, <u>preach</u>, saying, The kingdom of heaven is at hand. Heal the sick, cleanse the lepers, raise the dead, cast out devils: freely ye have received, freely give.**

Most of our churches today do not preach the Kingdom of God like Jesus did, and they have their own message which is why the church is not attended, honored, or respected anymore. Churches have no idea what a kingdom consist of, how it functions, how to receive it, or how to pursue it. Matthew 6:33 states, "But seek ye first the kingdom of God, and his righteousness; and all these things shall be added unto you." When we seek the Kingdom, what are we really looking for? The Kingdom simply is where a state or government has a king or queen as its head; anything conceived as constituting a realm or sphere of independent action or control; the kingdom of thought; a realm or province of nature, especially one of the three broad divisions of natural objects: the animal, vegetable, and mineral kingdoms.

Jesus is our King and we are citizens of His kingdom. He brought the government on His shoulder and Isaiah 9:6 states, "For unto us a child is born, unto us a Son is given: and the <u>government</u> shall be upon his shoulder: and His name shall be called Wonderful, Counsellor, The mighty God, The everlasting Father, The Prince of Peace."

He rules and reign from heaven above. We as ambassadors are supposed to represent our country, which is heaven down here on earth, because that's where we come from. As ambassadors we do and say what our King says, so if such things as lying, cheating, stealing, and killing, are not allowed in our country, heaven, we should not be satisfied with those things here on the earth. Thy will be done on the earth just like it is in heaven, this is our petition.

When we pray it is a formally drawn request that addresses the Father because He is the One in authority, so we are soliciting some favors, rights, mercies, or other benefits, but we do this in Jesus' name. When Jesus was crucified, buried, and raised from the dead, He alone earned, qualified, and deserved to have all power in heaven and on earth, but He breathed on His disciples which gave them power over all devils and diseases. Now they are to preach and repeat the same thing Jesus preached.

Kingdom Mindset On Earth

Kingdom Beliefs

1. Which son did God tell Abraham to offer as a sacrifice?
   a) Esau b) Jacob c) Isaac

2. Would God have sacrificed His son Jesus if Abraham didn't sacrifice his son?
   a) Yes b) No c) Maybe

3. God, the Father, is trying to get to world system today is the message about a _____ (Elohim), His _____ and their _____.

4. He sent _____ the _____ to get our minds ready for the coming of the One who would restore back to man what _____ lost in the beginning.

5. John's message was to _____ for the _____ of _____ was near.

6. When _____ saw Jesus he said, "Behold the _____ of _____.

7. Why did Jesus come?
   a) to preach the kingdom
   b) to preach is death burial and resurrection

8. Luke 4:43 states, And he said unto his disciples, I must _____ the _____ of _____ to other cities also: for therefore am I _____.

9. Matthew 6:3 states, But seek ye first the _____ of _____, and his _____; and all these things shall be added unto _____.

10. The Kingdom simply is where a state _____ or _____ having a king or _____ as its head.

11. As _____ we do and say what our _____ says.

Kingdom Mindset On Earth

Kingdom Notes

Chapter 7
The NEW Heaven and NEW Earth

God is going to get what He originally said He wanted, that is for mankind to be His kingdom of priests, and only Jesus would be the reigning King. In the book of Isaiah 65:17 He states, "For, behold, I create new heavens and a new earth: and the former shall not be remembered, nor come into mind." Then Isaiah 65:25 says, "The wolf and the lamb shall feed together, and the lion shall eat straw like the bullock: and dust shall be the serpent's meat. They shall not hurt nor destroy in all my holy mountain, saith the LORD. It will be peace like in the beginning." John the Revelator in Revelation 21:1 says, "And I saw a new heaven and a new earth: for the first heaven and the first earth were passed away; and there was no more sea." This question has been in my mind for such a long time when I was coming up in the religious sector, *if we were to die and go to heaven forever then Jesus would not be restoring us back to where Adam fell from*?

Adam lost dominion over the earth, not heaven. Also, if we would be in heaven forever who would be on the new earth? According to these scripture many churches' message don't add up with the scriptures. Matthew 25:34 states, "Then shall the King say unto them on his right hand, Come, ye blessed of my Father, inherit the kingdom prepared for you from the foundation of the world." When asked about these scripture many pastors who actually don't understand the kingdom that Jesus preached would say, "We will understand it better by and by!!!" I believe this is just another way of saying, I don't have an answer for you and I don't understand, but I can't let you know that. Many people including Christians have a misunderstanding and misconception about what God is doing and what heaven is really like. Read the book of Revelation, Chapters 21 and 22, it shows us in detail a picture of the new heaven and the new earth. Eternal life, the dwelling place for believers, will be the new earth. The new earth will be the new heaven where we are to spend eternity. This is what John saw and wrote. Even the holy city, the New Jerusalem, that came down from God is on the new earth where the streets of gold and the pearly gates will be.

  The new earth is a physical place where we will have our glorified body. First Corinthians 15:38-39 states, "But God giveth it a body as it hath pleased him, and to every seed his own body. All flesh is not the same flesh: but there is one kind of flesh of men, another flesh of beasts, another of fishes, and another of birds." The heaven that we as believers believe, will be the new planet that is made perfect by God like He wanted it in the beginning. We will have a new earth free from all sin, suffering, evil, killing, and death. Therefore, what John saw was a new universe.

This is the petition that we ask God for now: Thy kingdom come. Thy will be done on the earth just as it is in heaven.

In other words,
Father, Let Our Domain Look Like Yours!!!

Kingdom Beliefs

1. For, behold, I create new _____ and a new _____ and the former shall not be _____, nor come into mind. (Isaiah 65:17)

2. Adam lost _____ over the earth not _____.

3. If the Christians would be in _____ forever who would be on the new _____?

4. _____ life the _____ place for believers will be the new earth and not _____.

5. The new earth is a _____ place where the believers of Christ glorified body will be.

6. The new earth will be free from all sin, suffering, evil, killing babies, and death.
   __True __False

7. Will man live in heaven forever?
   __True __False

8. Will believers live on the new earth?
   __True   __False

9. Our petition to God is: For now Thy _____ come Thy will be _____ on the earth just as it is in _____.

Kingdom Mindset On Earth

Kingdom Notes

About the Author ...

Bishop Anthony L. Taylor, Sr. is the pastor of New Hope Church, located in North County, Missouri. He is the proud husband of Sis. Elaine Taylor, married for twenty-eight years, and the father of five. He is a man blessed with many gifts and talents: he preaches and teaches the Word of God with the profoundness of Kingdom Building, sings under the anointing of the Holy Spirit, plays several musical instruments, including the piano, organ, guitar, and drums. He taught music and Biblical Theology classes at The Glad Tidings Bible College. Bishop Taylor served on the board of Job for Justice in implementing minimum wage increase. He's a board member of the organization MOSES, a board member of the Universal Mission for Sickle Cell, and also a member of the World Global Network for Kingdom building, and assists in the public school in mentoring the youth.

Education

Bishop Taylor holds the following degrees:

- ✟ Bachelor Degree, Auto Mechanics
- ✟ Associate Degree, Theology
- ✟ Bachelor Degree, Biblical Theology
- ✟ Masters Degree, Religious Education

He became an Ordained Bishop in 2005, and has completed all credits required for a Doctrine Degree. Bishop Taylor is in the process of writing his dissertation.

His Vision

Bishop Taylor has accomplished many goals to be proud of in anyone's lifetime; however, out of all his accomplishments, he is most focused, thankful, and steadfast in the work of the Lord. He is definitely about Kingdom Building!!! The vision given by God to Bishop Taylor is to use God's principles for furthering kingdom building, preaching and teaching the plan for mankind to win as many souls as God allows; contributing and supporting missions near and abroad, which carries the message that Jesus Saves; establishing and implementing a youth ministry to reach not only the youth at New Hope Church, but also the youth of surrounding neighborhoods who may otherwise seek unfavorable alternatives in the streets.

About the Author

Accomplishments

✞ Traveled to Israel participating in the Peace Mission
✞ Traveled to London for Global Leadership Meetings
✞ Traveled to Greece, South Africa, Rome, and Nassau Bahamas all for building the Kingdom
✞ Real Estate Investor

Kingdom Notes

www.ingramcontent.com/pod-product-compliance
Lightning Source LLC
Chambersburg PA
CBHW071036080526
44587CB00015B/2640